Excel Power Query

Excel for Beginners

Table of Contents

Chapter 1

Excel Power Query Editor: Excel for Beginners

Introduction:

Microsoft, the tech giant, is known for its new innovative and user-friendly products.

While you would love the new products it has on offer, from the Surface Book to the Surface Studio, the one thing that most people can never forget is just how useful some of the Microsoft software is.

Who doesn't use Microsoft Word for one - even Mac users can't ignore its utility.

Businesses love Microsoft Excel for its ability to keep records – but as we shall see below, it goes a lot farther than just helping you stay up to date.

Microsoft Excel: A Look

Microsoft has now come out with an updated version of Excel 2010. The new version Microsoft Excel 2013 proves itself to be a lifesaver for the user, who wants loads of information just with one click. Both the new changing scenarios and the tech savvy world will look forward to this new product from Microsoft, which is basically made for quick accessibility.

Excel 2013 comes with many additions in terms of tools. The new program comes with the addition of the 'Touch Mode' Option. It also offers co authoring with the help of Sky Drive, along with the builtin sharing menu. A Flash feature introduced in this version of Excel will also help the user in many ways, for instance users can now keep an eye on what they have stored in a spreadsheet.

The Quick analysis tool, when selected, will expand itself into a selection box. Just by keeping the mouse held onto the selected option, the user gets a preview of any changes they have made. With the help of this tool users can modify the selected data however needed for things like ex- formatting, tables, spark lines, etc.

Excel 2013 gives the user an edge by placing before him these and other options which will give him enhanced accessibility.

The new version is much better from the previous one in all respects, however; collaboration features needs more refinment and innovation to be made by Microsoft.

User accessibility and simultaneous editing are now ready to blast open the software market along with the increased focus on the new Cloud technology. Microsoft's new version will score out in the market due to the above mentioned reasons.

Artificial Intelligence and Microsoft Excel

We are living in a time when Artificial Intelligence and Big Data rule the IT world. All the applications are so designed to need minimum human interference. This speeds up the processing time, as well as reduces the chances of human errors.

We are seeing a whole range of new programs dedicated specifically for automation of various applications. There is a sea of information in the virtual world which needs to be collected, sorted and analyzed. Doing this manually is neither possible nor an efficient way of doing so. To perform such tasks, there are a lot of dedicated applications like Hadoop and Azure performing big data analysis.

MS-Excel has always been associated with collection and analysis of data. With the ever-developing technology, MS-Excel Power Query was introduced to meet the new-age business demands. It comes with better technology for collecting data from various sources and their analysis for desired information.

Power Query is a free Excel-add-in meant for enhancing self-service business intelligence. It uses data across all big data software like Azure marketplace and OData and allows the analysts to make proper manipulations to them for a better analysis experience. This empowers them to make informed business decisions.

Today, the role of business analysts is mostly dependent upon these analytical tools. This enables them to give calculated advice and also proper risk-management for various projects.

1.1 Data analysis (Business Intelligence)

Having access to the right information at the right time gives power to organizations. Easy to use Business Intelligence tools create high value, while helping companies stay ahead of their competitors.

This means with its help, your organization can stay ahead of the competition by providing you the correct information at the right time with minimal effort. You don't have to worry about looking for data in multiple places, or learning complex SQL statements to find out the business information. You will find it easy to deal with an increasing number of reports, dashboards and natural-language query engines which can be used by business users without any technical support.

In this digital world, every business generates tons of data, that needs to be collected, cleaned, related (to each other), stored in a central place and most importantly, it should be accessible to business users via an easy interface. Converting data to valuable information is a key success factor in helping organizations make the right decisions.

You must have noticed that you begin to get advertisements on your web browsers which actually are related to your previous web searches. How does that happen? Let us explain that with an example. You searched on Google for best management courses across the country. This information went into the virtual world of cyberspace, and after analysis by various AI and Big data software, it was concluded that you might be interested in a particular college or a course. But, other colleges don't want to lose out.

They also want to attract your attention. Your IP address is traced by these AI and Big Data software used by the colleges and, you begin to receive notifications regarding various management colleges. These institutes utilize the technology to attract your attention. This is a very small example of how business intelligence works.

There are scores of applications that efficiently sort out the information from web space and then uses it for business purposes. Imagine the scores of business flourishing in cyberspace just because of these two technical advancements.

Business intelligence allows the decision makers to make informed decisions. These, in turn, pave the way to better business plans, better execution and ultimately increased revenue.

Often we come across a reputed brand entering a new business. Do they enter on their whims and fancies? No.

Their decision makers and analysts first thoroughly study that particular market. They select the niche for themselves. Let us explain it with an example. There is some company X. If they are venturing into the clothing business, their analysts determine if it would be profitable to be specific for men, women and kids or just for plus sized people. Currently, not many companies manufacture plus sized clothes.

So, company X will have very few competitors. And, if they analyze the market and fashion trends, the company X is bound to succeed.

This data analysis was not so profound a few years back. Most of the nations were closed economies and their domestic markets had only a few players. But with most of the nations becoming open economies today, the competition for each and every segment of the market has increased dramatically.

Just for a small thing like a toothbrush, we have now more than 500 companies, including domestic and MNCs.

In such severe competition, a good business analyst needs the backing of an efficient data analytic tool. Power Query fills this gap and empowers business analysts to function efficiently.

Business intelligence software ensures all these analytical tasks are accurately conducted, and hence, they are a major factor in success stories. They enable the policy makers to collect the data and sort it to suit their needs.

1.2 Power Query

While analyzing a set of data, one needs to first collect it from various sources. These sources contain data like tables, graphs pie charts, etc. One needs to study them carefully and then mould them into another analytical representation. Microsoft Power BI self-service solution introduced Power Query as an add-in to ease this process.

With its interactive user interface, Power Query allows users to search, detect, sort, associate, convert and modify data as well. A business decision maker needs to gather information from various sources across the Internet. Power Query can be easily used for searching such stats.

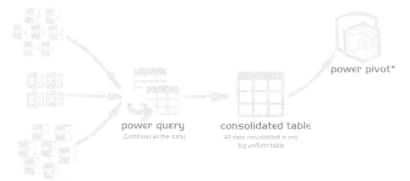

power pivot*

power query
(Combines all the data)

consolidated table
All data consolidated in one
big uniform table

* Optional direct load of the consolidated table to Power Pivot
Note: Power Query can handle all the desired file types at the same time or you can always filter the steps to only handle a certain file type.

The best part of Power Query is that it allows importing from any data source. Some of the data sources are:

a. Web sources

b. CSV, XML, Excel, any folder with metadata and links

c. SQL Server, Oracle, IBM DB2, MySQL, Windows Azure SQL Database

d. SharePoint list, Windows Azure Blob Storage, Facebook and so on.

So why is PowerQuery so much in demand?

We need to realize today's world heavily depends on utilizing each and every second. The business analysts have a very important role in ensuring their concerned business functions properly. In this vast world, an analysis is always needed.

However, analysts had to work pretty hard, to get something that was not worth their time. Even if they needed to compare two sets of data, they had to spend too much time doing it. Their potential was getting wasted. They had to copy-paste data from one source to the Excel sheets.

Then there was the need to manually arrange them, analyze them and derive the results. It was realized that there was a dearth of an automation tool which would especially target the business enterprises. PowerQuery is the brainchild of this demand. By using PowerQuery, the business analysis has become very simple and time efficient.

Those analysts who had to spend two to three hours in just organizing and analyzing data can now do so in a matter of minutes. Their potential can now be fully utilized. Also, the process has become error-proof and faster.

PowerQuery has truly revolutionized the business enterprise.

1.3 Why should you use PowerQuery?

Everyone is going mad over PowerQuery. It is the hottest technology right now. Everyone wants to learn it. But what is so different about it? Why should you invest your time in learning this new software? Isn't it just an extension of MS-Excel?

We have got answers to all your questions. Yes, PowerQuery is actually an add-in for MS-Excel. And, it is totally worth your time. In fact, it will save you a lot of time. If you do any of the following jobs, you should learn this as soon as possible:

a. Collecting data manually from various sources.

b. Creating Excel sheets and feeding data manually

c. Analyzing and interpreting data

d. Cross-checking data to ensure it is error-proof.

e. Reshape data for the correct Excel format

f. Write too many Vlookups every day to combine tables.

All these work together with many new functions can be easily performed with just PowerQuery.

Data collection, organization and analysis are completely automated with this. You only need to feed the data sources; the rest will be done by the software. In short, you can perform following functions comfortably with the use of Power Query.

a. Discover data across various platforms

b. Find connections between seemingly unrelated data sets

c. Import data sets from various external, as well as internal sources.

d. Create custom tables, columns for your data

e. Merge, add, delete or reshape the tables. You can even rename them.

f. Create a new query from two queries.

g. Create data visualizations for big data platforms

h. Share queries online and also among your colleagues

This will save you from useless effort and save you lots of time. Just imagine your efficiency when you will not have to do the lethargic work of manually analyzing the different datasets!

Chapter 2

Getting started with Power Query

Power Query may not be present in every Excel version, especially in Excel 2010.

Here, we will guide you on how to install it. In Excel 2016, it is known as Get & Transform. PowerQuery is so efficient everyone related to an analytical job should learn it. With just basic Excel skills, one can perform refined functions with different sets of data quite easily.

They no longer have to rely on other professionals to get their work done. They can do so easily on their own computer setup. Also, the data generated is accurate and you get many options to modify it. However, one also should try to learn M language. This is not necessary, but knowing it will only increase your skill set.

M language is used in the coding of Power Query. So, if you know M language, you can also create custom functions for the Power Query for your data usage.

2.1 Installing Power Query

Pre-requisites for installing Power Query:

1. MS Office 2013 Professional Plus

2. Office 365 ProPlus

3. Excel 2013 standalone

4. MS Office 2010 Professional Plus with Software Assurance

You need to have any one of these.

2.2 Step by Step way to install Power Query

1. Go to https://www.microsoft.com/en-us/download/details.aspx?id=39379&CorrelationId=80a61fd2-635f-4fb9-acf2-7fdcae613ebb

2. At the end of the page, you will get a download icon. But, you should first read the details, system requirements, install instructions and related resources. This will allow you to smoothly install Power Query.

3. After clicking download, you will get a screen like this:

4. Select the version you wish to download by ticking in the box.

5. Now, click on "next" button.

6. Open the setup wizard icon and install Power Query.

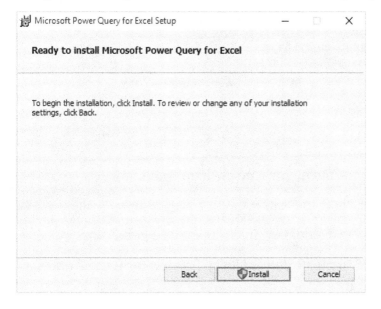

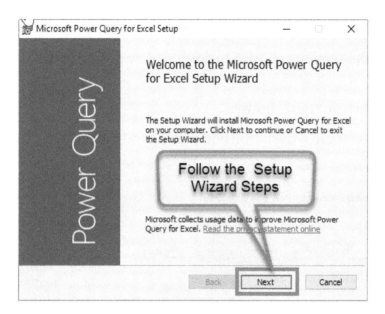

7. Now go to "file menu" and click on" options."

8. Click on "add-ins" tab

9. Select "COM Add-Ins" from "manage combo" box.

10. Select Microsoft Power Query Preview for Excel from COM Add-Ins.

11. Power Query tab then appears in Excel and is ready to be used.

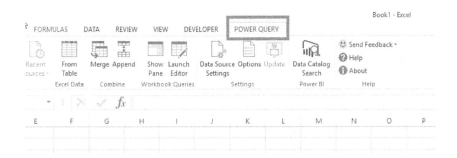

Chapter 3

Query sharing

What is query sharing?

People often construct various queries regarding their business in Excel. It could be for sales figures, profit and loss and so on. These sets of data may be merged for a new query. These queries are useful for other employees for the company and even serve as an online resource. Their collection and analysis are usually time-taking. Hence, it is wiser to share them for others to use. When the queries constructed are shared this way, it is known as query sharing.

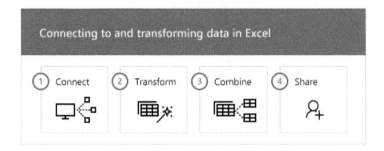

It is very common for the companies to use the older queries for training their new staff. In the absence of this query sharing feature, it was really difficult for the new employees to understand the tid-bits of this technology. But, query sharing also acts as training material by storing every step of the operation.

Trainees or new employees can learn by studying every subsequent step just with a few clicks. Hasn't PowerQuery changed the face of the business analytics by making it time-efficient, error-proof and also great as a training material?

How does Power Query help in query sharing?

Power Query saves the data, as well as the steps involved in acquisition and analysis and also saves the generated report in the Power Query formula language. In short, it automates the whole process involved in query creation. These steps can be easily accessed through the "advanced editor" tab under the "view" tab.

3.1 Sharing a query in Power Query

In order to share your query with others in Power Query, you need to follow these simple steps:

1. Sign into Power BI for Office 365 in MS-Excel.

2. Select the table or data that you wish to share.

3. Click on the "query" tab that is on the right side of the screen.

4. Now, click on "share."

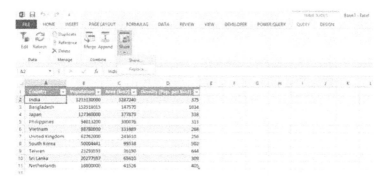

5. Now the shared query will appear in search results when any user online searches for this query.

3.2 How do you import data from external sources?

There are times when you would need data from various sources. It could be from the Azure database of your own company or some type of online databases. You can use Power Query to import data from all sorts of external sources quite conveniently. The steps are as below:

1. Open MS-Excel home page.

2. Click on "data" icon

3. Choose the source from which you want to import data.

4. "From access" allows you to import data from the MS-Access Database.

5. "From web" lets you to import data from the Web.

When you click this icon, you will get a dialogue box to fill in the web URL you wish to visit. After that, click on "import."

6. By choosing "from text," you can import data from a text file.

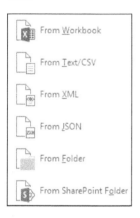

7. "From other sources" allows you to import data from other data sources that are:

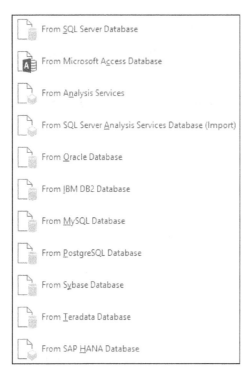

a. SQL Server

b. Analysis Services

c. XML data import

d. Data connection wizard & OLEDB

e. Microsoft query wizard & ODBC

8. If you select "existing connections," you will get a list of your commonly used data sources to choose from.

3.3 Understanding Query Editor

Query Editor enables you to modify and operate various data-related operations over a data source. You can add or subtract data tables and/or data types. You can perform various addition-deletions to rows and columns too. Query Editor creates instructions for these operations in the M language.

Power Query Editor Window
These buttons automate common processes!

Query Editor is an integral part of the Power BI and hence of the power query. Most of the data analysts use this part for the achieving the desired manipulations of the data acquired from various sources.

The language of the Query Editor

The programming language behind Power Query is Power Query Formula Language, also known as M language. Here, M represents Data Mashup or Data modelling. It is a mashup query language.

Like all other programming languages, it has its own set of structure and syntax. Because it is currently new and not so wide-spread, people usually maintain a distance from it. Additionally, its use for editing in Power Query, which is itself a new program right now, adds to the skeptics. But, as a matter of fact, this is an easy to understand program with pretty easy syntaxes. Here we will explain the different components of the M language.

M's syntax:

M language consists of two programming blocks, namely LET expression block and In expression block.

M language has different function categories. Some of them are:

- Date functions
- Error handling
- List functions
- Duration functions
- Accessing data functions
- Combiner functions
- Action functions
- Uri functions
- Splitter functions
- Logical functions
- And so on...

Chapter 4

Functions using Query Editor

Suppose you have procured a set of data from the Internet that consists of several columns and rows. But, you have different needs. Like, you need data from only two rows and columns and wish to merge data from another table. All these functions can be easily performed in the Query Editor.

Query Editor has distinct functions for rows and columns. Let us have a look at both individually.

4.1 Column Functions

When you have a data set, you may need to add, delete or modify the columns in it. Power Query enables you to:

a. Delete columns

b. Split or merge columns

c. Add custom columns

d. Sort and filter columns

e. Analyze cumulative data

f. Unpivot available data for pivot tables

To do that, you need to follow these steps:

1. Go to Power Query

2. Select "edit;" it will automatically take you to Query Editor.

3. In the Home tab, you get "manage columns."

a. You can choose columns here

b. You can delete one or more columns by selecting "remove columns."

c. You can rename a particular column by selecting "rename."

d. You can change the position of a particular column by using "move" option.

4. Under "transform,, you will find different set of functions.

a. You can sort the columns according to a particular criterion by using "group by." This can be particularly helpful when you are dealing with different types of tables and wish to find some pattern in them.

b. You can also pivot or unpivot columns here.

c. You can split column(s) by selecting the option.

5. Under the "add column," you can find the below options:

a. You can custom create a column to include the data of your interest

b. You can also add an index column to keep track of your rows of numbers in the data.

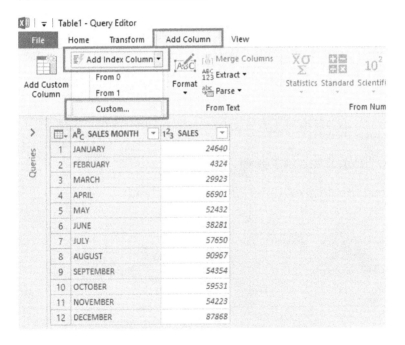

c. Using "duplicate column," you can create a copy of selected column(s).

d. You can also merge two or more columns by selecting the "merge columns" option.

e. If you wish to change the format of your column, you can do so by selecting "format."

4.2 Row Functions You can also perform many functions with the rows in your data. Most of them work in the same way as the column functions. Here, we have explained them in these steps:

1. Go to "home" tab in Power Query

2. Choose the desired function under the "reduce row" ribbon.

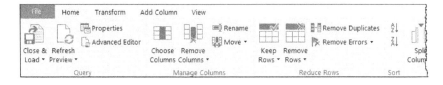

3. Under the "transform" tab, you can do following operations:

a. Use the first row as the header in the data

b. Transpose, reverse and count rows

4.2 Transforming a query

When you are dealing with large datasets, you never know how you may have to shape the data to make it worth your usage. As for example, you have a table that shows the year, production cost, profit, employee number, employee salary and expenses of a company. However, you need to work with only employee numbers and employee salaries. All other columns are of no use to you. So, you need to delete them.

You can perform many other functions in a similar way. Let us give you an example:

1. Select "PowerQuery" tab.

2. Select get external data; select from the file; select Excel.

3. You will get a list of Excel files on your system.

4. Now, select the one on which you want to perform the operation.

5. When you select that, a navigator pane will open on the right side of the screen.

6. Select the table which you want to reshape.

7. Then select "edit."

8. The query editor will appear on the screen as a pop-up window.

9. Select the properties that you want to change.

10. After making changes, click on "close" and "load."

11. The changes made by you will appear in the new query.

In these simple steps, you can reshape the way data is presented in the tables. You can make the presentation more crisp and to-the-point. And at the top of it, all the relationships will be correctly established.

4.3 Refreshing a query

There are times when the tables or the query generated need to be updated constantly. Like, if you have made a query on a particular Facebook page visits, then this statistic will change every hour. Many companies like the online shopping sites, have to keep a close watch on the number of visits on their website. Such sites derive their income from them. But, it will be a very tedious process if someone needed to update the query every hour. Also, the chances of error will be high.

To prevent such errors and time-loss, there is a feature called refresh query in the query editor. All you need to do is choose the function required and then refresh it. Any new data added or updated will be automatically updated in this query.

The simple steps;

1. Go to Query Editor

2. Click "refresh preview"

3. The query will be automatically updated

4.4 Filter a table

Get some undesirable data. Even useless data needs to be filtered out for a good PowerQuery Excel sheet. Else, it will become very confusing to look at even the un-related rows and columns in the Excel sheet. There are several options to filter a column. We have explained some of them briefly here;

1. Text filter: This is very similar to the "find" option. You can sort out the text data by filtering it with the words they contain or lack. Like, if there are many words beginning with R, but you want to find those which don't begin with R, then you can put the text filter as: "not beginning with R." All such words will automatically get sorted out. The steps involved are:

a. Select the column(s) to be filtered.

b. Select the down arrow at the top of the column name

c. Select "text filters."

d. You will get a menu containing filter options:

- Equals
- Does not equal
- Begins with
- Does not begin with
- Ends with
- Does not end with
- Contains
- Does not contain

e. Select the filter you wish to apply.

f. Select "OK."

g. Text filter will sort out the text data according to the filter applied.

2. Auto filter

If you want to just default filter the columns of your table, you can select the auto-filter option. It can be applied in following ways;

a. For applying the auto-filter

b. There is a down arrow just beside the column name. Click it.

c. Select the auto-filter values that you want to apply.

d. Select "OK."

e. Your query will be filtered according to the filters applied by you.

3. Number or date/time filters

Suppose you own a café. You want to monitor the time and day when your café has the highest footfall. For this, you need to have the number of customers that visited your café on a particular day. You can easily get the time and date and subsequently the number from your bill database. Now, you need to sort out the number of people present on a particular day and at a particular time.

For such scenarios, Power Query has a different filter that sorts out the columns according to number, date and time. Let us see the steps in which you can use this feature:

a. Select the column over which you want to apply this filter.

b. Select the down arrow.

c. Among the options that you will get, select number filters or date/time filters.

d. Click "OK."

e. The filter will give you the analysis of how many people visited your café on a particular day.

f. You can also have a comparative study by clicking on the equality type filter. You can then make out the days on which you have maximum and minimum customers.

4. Filter column(s) by row position

When you deal with external data sheets, you get several unwanted rows. As for example, you have a data-sheet for past 10 years, but you need only info for the last 2 years. In this case, you have to filter out the top 8 rows. However, this may not always be the case. To make this easier, there are many customized options in Power Query. You have the following options for filtering rows:

a. Keep top 100 rows

• Select the "table" icon

• Select "keep top 100 rows."

• Top 100 rows from your data sheet will be filtered out.

b. Keep top rows: Here, you have to manually enter the number of rows from the top to keep.

• Right click on the "table" icon.

• You will get a dialog box

• Select "keep top rows" option.

• Enter the number of rows from top which you want to keep.

• The filter will sort out the top X number of rows.

c. Remove top rows: It is helpful when you have smaller number of unwanted rows to remove. The steps involved are:

• Right click on the "table" icon.

• You will again get a dialog box demanding the number of rows to be removed.

• Enter the number of rows that you want to remove.

• Always pay attention that this instruction says remove top rows. You should always fill in the number of rows from the top.

d. Remove alternate rows: Suppose you want to have data for the alternate years or months or whatever columns. Manually removing the alternate rows can be a tiring process. To make this work easier, you should use "remove alternate rows" option. The steps involved are:

• Right click on the table icon.

• Select "remove alternate rows."

• You will get a dialog box.

• In this box, fill in the first row number to be removed, total number of rows to be removed and also the total number of rows to keep. This ensures that the wrong sequence of rows is not deleted. Also, when you count the total number of rows to be kept and removed, it helps you in tracking the filtered rows.

e. Keep range of rows: sometimes you may need to sort out the rows according to their range. This feature comes handy then. The steps involved are:

• Right click on the "table" icon.

• Select "keep range of rows."

• You will get a dialog box demanding the ranges to be kept.

• Enter the first row number and the total number of rows to be kept.

• Select "OK."

• The filter will sort out the data according to the range you have applied.

There are several other functions that can be performed by Query Editor. The other notable functions are:

• Sort a table according to different criteria or in ascending or descending order.

• Group rows of a table according to their values into a single row.

• Get cumulative data from table(s) for analyzing group operations like addition, subtraction.

• Expand a column that contains the required table

• Insert a custom made column into a table

• Merge several queries to create a new query

• Edit steps of query in advanced editor. You should know M language for performing this.

• Split columns

• Insert a new query into the Excel worksheet

• Remove selected column(s) from a query... and the list goes on.

Power Query basically has all the functions options needed by the analysts.

4.5 Utilizing Query Editor

Today there are several multi-national firms in the market. Together with that, even the small and medium scale businesses are trying to automate their whole process. This saves them with time and also manpower. The work which previously needed three to four accountants can now be finished in half the time by anyone well-versed in Power Query. This has accelerated the business operations and increased the efficiency of the work-force. Also, the companies are now able to get better data stats with less manpower.

Query Editor is actually more than just an editor. You can perform a whole lot of functions to improve the data you have collected.

Get proper manipulations in a meaningful manner and with absolutely zero errors. The best part of Query Editor is that anyone with the sound knowledge of MS-Excel can perform all these operations.

You can also use R programming language in Query Editor for further data cleansing and more sophisticated data output.

The only tricky part for the novices can be inserting functions. This requires practice. Also, if you want to customize the query instructions, you need to know the M language.

Chapter 5

Power Pivot

Power Pivot is basically an analytical tool (SQL Server Analysis Services Engine) for polishing the data received from Power Query. It was first introduced in Excel 2010 as an add-in. It can perform operations on millions of rows in a single Excel sheet at once.

And the best part is that these data can be from different sources. So, you can import any kind and any amount of data from Facebook or Twitter and simultaneously perform various manipulations and analysis in a single Excel sheet. We can say that is basically the upgraded version of Excel. Excel can't handle this amount of data in a single sheet. Using Power Pivot, you can:

a. Establish a relationship between different tables

b. Arrange them in gradations

c. Establish properties of rows and columns

d. Create "key performance indicators."

e. Add suitable formulae with data analysis expressions.

Data Analysis Expressions (DAX) is the programming language used for Power Pivot. Anyone who uses power BI should know Power Pivot. Especially those who are involved in the data analysis field should learn it for their own use.

However, Power Pivot is available built-in only in Excel 2013 & 2016. If you wish to install Power Pivot add-in, you should follow these steps:

1. Go to "file" in Excel

2. Select "options"

3. Select "Add-ins."

4. You will get a managed box; in its drop-down menu select "COM Add-Ins."

5. Click "go."

6. Tick mark the box that states "Microsoft power pivot for Excel."

7. Click "OK."

5.1 Merge Query

Suppose you have prepared two tables for your garment company. One table contains the total cost of production in last ten years along with profits earned. Another table contains the areas where your company has showed the maximum growth. Now, you wish to merge both these tables to establish the relationship between the profits and new market area gained by your company.

Many times, you get two large data sets that have one or two columns of your interest. But manually extracting data from those four columns can be very time-taking and prone to human errors. You can simplify the task by using merge function of the power query. It allows you to select the columns for merger and merges them very conveniently. You will get a new query that will contain columns from both tables merged to give you the perfect set of data needed.

You can easily perform this using the "merge query" tab. You can perform two types of merges:

a. Intermediate merge: With each merge performed, a new query will be generated.

b. Inline merge: Using this, you can merge the whole table into your table. You can continue doing this until you reach your desired result.

Here, we will explain in steps, how to perform a merge:

1. Go to Power Query tab.

2. Select "merge" under the combined tab.

3. You will get a dialog box on your screen.

4. Select the primary table for merge from the drop-down list. Usually, the active query is taken as the primary table.

5. Select a column from the column header

6. Selected the secondary table or the table that you wish to merge with the first one.

7. Select the column from the column header that matches with this table.

8. When you are making multiple merges, you need to make sure that the number of columns selected in the primary and secondary (relatable) tables is same. If not, an additional dialog box will appear informing you of a failed merge.

9. Select "only include matching rows" to include only intersecting rows from both the tables. If you fail to tick this dialog box, all the rows from the primary table will get included in the resultant query. This may not always be desirable.

10. Click "OK."

11. You get a new query created out of the data from both tables.

This can be performed in another way too. The steps are:

12. Go to Power Query tab

13. Click on the "show pane" option

14. Right-click on the "orders" query

15. Select reference from the list of options

16. This will create a new query. Right-click on the new query and select "edit."

17. Select the "merge" button in the Power Query editor.

18. The selected tables will be merged.

However, the earlier explained method is more convenient.

5.2 Multiple Joins (Vlookup)

Vlookup is basically for performing look-up function. Like a phone directory, it sorts out data in a particular pattern. Following that pattern, you can easily find the data you need. You need to enter the vlookup() in functions bar to get the unknown data that you want to extract from the set of available data.

Using Power Pivot, you can also merge multiple tables. The only requirement for this is to create a meaningful relationship between the columns of the multiple tables.

Here are the steps to perform multiple joins in power pivot using Vlookup.

1. Select the Excel cell where you wish to have the desired value.

2. Write =Vlookup() in functions row.

3. Fill the parenthesis as (column where the desired result is needed, a range of cells containing data that you search, column number, true/false). Always put comma and colon between the values. Otherwise, Vlookup does not process the function.

4. Put "false" to get an exact match and "true" for an approximate match. "True" is the default option.

5. Press "enter."

Points to be noted:

a. While putting in a range, always put the colon between the two values. Like, if the look up value begins from the B2 cell and ends in F12, then your range should be B2: F12. The absence of a colon will not allow the function to run.

b. Always ensure that the data in the first column of the table array is a not a text. Otherwise, the function will return an error message.

c. Always use absolute references for range-lookup.

There is another way for merging columns. The steps are:

1. Select the Excel workbook

2. Navigate to the column you want to merge

3. Select "merge" from "query" tab

4. You will get a dialog box

5. Select the primary table()the one with the value you want to keep

6. Then select the relatable query

7. You will get a new expandable column.

8. Select "organizational" from the privacy levels dialog box.

9. This will give your both data sources, privacy.

10. Select "save."

11. Select "OK,"

12. Both the tables will be merged. And, you will get a new query with both the merged columns.

5.3 How is Power Pivot different from Excel?

Till now, we have seen that the functions performed by power pivot are more or less similar to the functions performed by Excel. So, why is there so much emphasis on learning Power Pivot when we already are very comfortable with Excel?

Actually, both of these programs may seem similar, but there are some basic differences between the two. In order for you to appreciate the importance of both of these separately, you need to know the difference that puts them apart.

The difference can be observed in the programming language of both of them and their syntaxes.

Power Pivot functions always need some argument that consists of expressions or tables or values. These functions always begin with a = sign and are followed by any scalar expression. This scalar expression can be +, -, * and so on. Usually, Excel language utilizes arrays or sets of values as functions but Power Pivot utilizes tables and inputs for the same function.

In Excel, you can perform functions on particular cells or columns separately. You don't need to perform the function on the entire table or column. But, in the case of Power Pivot, you need to include the entire column or table in the operation.

Chapter 6

Conditional Functions

Power Query works with a set of functions that are case sensitive. Also, they need to be filled in a particular pattern. Otherwise, you will get a null result. "If" is lowercase in Power Query and should not be confused with "IF" function of Excel.

Here we have explained how to perform Power Query "if" statements.

1. Go to Query Editor.

2. Select "add column" tab.

3. Now select the "conditional" column.

4. Fill up the new column name.

5. Fill up the subsequent fields.

6. Click "OK."

We will be explaining important functions here.

6.1 Expression functions

You may need to deal with text values for many of your queries. They are usually tricky to handle. Here is a list of the expression functions that will help you to handle them.

a. Expression. Identifier: This can be used to get a text value that can be further used as an identifier from a text value.

b. Expression. Evaluate: This function analyses a text value and returns the result.

c. Expression. Constant: This returns a constant literal text from the value.

6.2 Table Functions

M language is used for scripting the functions in Power Query. In Power Query, tables are the backbone of the data. But you may need to perform certain operations on them to make them meet your needs. You have to just insert the proper function in the box. Here, we have mentioned some table functions for reference.

1. For table construction:

a. Table. View: This creates or extends a table according to the handlers defined by the user and also the customized action operations.

b. Table. FromRecords: This function lets a table be returned from a list of data.

c. Table. FromColumn: This forces a table to return from a list that consists of nested lists and also the names and values of the columns.

2. For information on the tables:

a. Table.RowCount: This counts the number of rows in a table.

b. Table.Schema: This gives a new table that contains the column description of the selected table.

c. Table. ColumnCount: This counts the number of columns present in a specified table.

3. For conversions in tables or of the tables:

a. Table. ToRecord: This function gives a list of records from an input table as the output.

We have similar functions for table information, row operations and column operations.

Chapter 7:

Examples

We have explained enough of the various functions of Power Query. Now, let us demonstrate how they work with two examples. In the first example, we have explained how to make an invoice data so even the small businesses can benefit very much from using Power Query. They can plan strategically and can get expert like income sheets to attract investors.

In the second example, we have given an example of a payroll statement. It is very common for the companies to project the growth of their employees in a fixed duration of time.

7.1 Invoice data

What is invoice data?

. Invoice data is actually the data you get along with an invoice. Power Query actually works to extract the useful set of information from these invoices.

As for example, a company generated 50 invoices in a month. Now, this invoice generation means the company managed to sell 50 products in that particular month. You can now derive the profit gained for that month. With other Power Query tools, you can compare or contrast them with other months. You can also predict the market growth scenario. Just by using Power Query you get a whole new field to play.

Here are the steps of creating invoice data using PowerQuery:

1. Open the Excel sheet from which you want to generate the data.

2. Now select Power Query.

3. Select the columns you want to generate an invoice from.

4. Select "transform."

5. Select "group by."

6. In the dialog box generated, fill the group by part with the distinguishing feature you need to use. It could be sales year or total profit; anything from the datasheet.

7. Fill in the new column name

8. Select "operation" from the drop-down menu.

9. The operations are the sum, average, median, minimum, maximum, count rows, count distinct rows and all rows.

10. Select the one that you need to perform.

11. Select the "column" option. You will get options to choose from the columns that you had selected in Step 3.

12. Select "ok."

13. You will get a unique list.

14. Go to the "home" tab.

15. Select "close" and "load to" option.

16. You will get a dialog box giving you options for loading columns.

17. Select "load to a table."

18. Then select "new worksheet."

19. Click "load."

20. You will get a separate invoice data which you can even merge with the original data.

7.2 Payroll Statement

Suppose you have ten employees working for you. You have their monthly salary statements. Now, you want to estimate their salary growth for next 24 months. How will you do it?

Here, are the steps to perform this interesting task in PowerQuery:

1. Open the Excel sheet with employees' names and current salary.

2. Add a column that states "increase" and add expected percentage increase under it.

3. Fill in the cells with expected salary after performing the required function in the function tab.

4. Perform the above-mentioned steps for each of the ten employees.

5. Now you get a query table.

6. Go to Query Editor.

7. Under query settings, fill in the name column.

8. In your case, it should be monthly salary.

9. Choose "applied steps."

10. You will get three options:

a. Unpivot other columns

b. Renamed columns

c. Changed type 1

11. Choose category option from the screen

12. Choose unpivot other columns from the drop-down menu

13. Now choose "attribute column."

14. Select "rename columns" from the query settings.

15. Rename attribute to month. You will get a numerical value for each of the months.

16. Select "monthly increase query" and refresh it.

17. Rename the second table generated.

18. In the functions column, write

=Table.RowCount(monthly increase)

19. Create a custom column by putting in the following instruction:

=List.Generate(() =>

[Month = 0, Salary125],

Each [Month]

Each [Month=[Month] + 1,
Salary=[Salary]*(1+MonthlyIncrease{[Month=[Month]+1]}[
Value])])

20. You will get a customized column.

21. Go to the "home" tab.

22. Now select "manage parameters' and then 'new parameters."

23. Give a new name to the parameter and fill in the other columns like put a decimal in the value option.

24. When you change the parameter, you can also change the function from the drop-down menu.

25. Select "create function." It will appear in the drop-down menu when you will select the new query generated.

26. Select "OK."

27. Now, select "add column."

28. Select 'invoke the custom function.'

29. You will get a dialog box. Fill in the new column name, function query and fill in the other details.

30. Click "OK."

31. You will get a list which you can expand to new rows.

32. You will get the desired table.

The significance of Power Query in both these examples

Both these examples depict a typical usage of Power Query for performing business-related analytics. It can be seen from the example that how power query helps any business organization for performing certain analysis, specific to their need helping them to reach informed and accurate decisions.

Power Query is a tool which is the answer to all those scenarios which in its absence would have taken much more time and effort reaching the same conclusion. In the first example, a cafe owner was able to analyze the number of people who visited his shop in the entire month. He is now able to make much better-informed decisions.

For example, he found that he had maximum foot-fall on Sundays between 4 pm-7pm. Now, he can arrange for more staff for this time slot that would cater to the needs of the customers. Also, he can arrange for more sitting area for these 3 hours. To attract even parents with kids, a small crèche inside the cafe will be perfect.

More coffee flavours and some discount for this limited time will be the perfect attraction for many. All these will ultimately lead to weigh more profit than he was previously making. All of this can be attributed to one informed decision of his. That is using Power Query to analyse the customer flow for an entire month.

Just imagine the effect that this kind of analysis and the subsequent informed business decisions can have on bigger and multi-national companies. pave the way for companies, big or small, are pitching for the inclusion of artificial intelligence software for their operational functions.

Chapter 8

Advance Features of Power Query

Advance features of Power Query enables the user to write complex queries according to their needs. You can use Power Query to create advanced queries. These queries use the Power Query formula language which can be used to build complex operations. Given below is the image depicting option from where this advance feature of Power Query can be used.

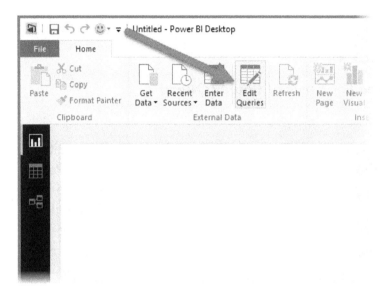

Here are the steps to perform advanced queries in the Power Query:

1. Go to "data" tab.

2. Select "get data"

3. Select "from other sources."

4. Select "blank query"

5. Select Query Editor

6. Now, select the "advanced editor."

7. You will get a note-pad like a screen showing the existing query code. You can change the codes to customize the editor.

8. Power Query uses M language. So, you need to be well versed in it.

9. After you have finished the coding, click on "done."

10. Now, select a file from Query Editor menu.

11. Select "close" and "apply."

12. Your code will be applied to the queries.

8.1 Scope of Power Query

With each passing day, the business organizations are moving from brick and mortar structures to online spaces. This space provides them with a vast area to explore without the red-tape associated with traditional business enterprises.

These days, we get lots of people who are looking into the field of data analysis as their career. As a matter of fact, in the coming times, many career options will become obsolete just because of the increased role of data analysts. Big Data and Artificial intelligence are the key to the future.

With Power Query, one gets command over Big Data lying in the large pool called the Internet. Extracting data associated with anything is now very easy. All you need to know is any Big Data programming like Hadoop or Azure. After that, you can extract data from whatever field you wish.

But only data extraction can never be the key to success. One also needs to properly compile and sort them to suit their needs. What will a garment industry do with the data related to automobile tires? Nothing! Exactly, in the same way, one needs to sort out the data of use and discard the ones that are of no significance.

PowerQuery allows this refinement and manipulation of the data. You can create several new queries from a single table to cater to your different needs. If you wish to operate on only some parts of the data-sheets, you can easily delete rows and columns. If you are familiar with the M programming language, you can even make customized query functions.

According to the recent trends in the market, being unfamiliar to the Power Query will prove to be career limiting. As a matter of fact, many people are simply now unsuitable for IT jobs because of their unfamiliarity with the Big Data and Artificial Intelligence software.

Those who are familiar with Power Query can present well-organized and nicely analyzed data. This is always a big demand for all the firms. So, how exactly does Power Query lead to well-organized data? Here are a few points:

a. You can find and merge the same data accumulated from different sources. Thus, you will get rid of duplicates.

b. You can edit the faults in the data and put in the correct values. This will simply eliminate the confusion arising out of different values for the same data.

c. You can even create customized queries to suit your different needs.

d. You can perform several edits, sorts, renaming and likewise functions on whatever number of tables you wish to do.

People need to come out of the mentality that Excel has limited functions. Today, it has more functions than any other specialised data analytics tool. The efficiency and accuracy provided by Power Query are unmatched.

And, the only thing that one needs to learn separately is M language. I would suggest that people should learn it for making maximum utilization of Power Query. It will also enable them to be more efficient with their data analytics task.

Who should use Power Query?

People are way too confused about the usage of Power Query. Ask anyone and they would ask you back that why they should use Power Query when they are already using Excel. Now, they need to be told that Power Query is not a replacement forExcel. In fact, it is an add-in or it. In other words, Power Query is an extension of Excel for more efficient handling of a large amount of data.

So, who should use it more often?

a. Anyone involved with business decision making. These people need to deal with the unusually large amount of data that expands over a wide field. If they are not provided with any artificial intelligence software to ease their work, their true potential will be consumed in manually handling the data.

If these people will use Power Query, they will be able to extract a large amount of sorted data from the cyberspace.

Their analysis and further course of action will be much in sync with the market demand.

Ultimately, the company will benefit. Otherwise, if these data analysis functions are performed manually, it will mean more time taken and also more chances of human errors. These can severely lower the quality of the analysis. But, software like Power Pivot can ease these complexities and pave the way for more concise and precise data.

b. Anyone dealing with incorrect data: Not only business analysts, even the small businesses are nowadays using data analytics tools to further expand their business. These establishments may not always have a proper business analyst. But owing to the user-friendly interface of power query, anyone fluent with the MS-Excel can easily handle the data analytics.

They can utilize these tools for editing the wrong queries and even for editing the data sheets to suit their needs.

If a firm needs data on the population of a place and number of bread packets consumed, they can conveniently delete the columns that depict consumption of flour and rice. This seamless editing capacity allows every business owner to get a better grasp of the data of their company.

They can use it for their business outlook and better decision making.

c. A newbie in the IT field: Newbies need to keep themselves equipped with the latest technologies to attract the recruiters more.

Learning Power Query is the best shot for them right now. They will be able to analyze and modify the company's data very efficiently.

Since Power Query is what we can call artificial intelligence and big data combined; it is going to affect things for a very long time. In fact, even the experienced IT professionals should learn it. It would help them in easing their workload and also in remaining updated with the recent technologies.

Future of Power Query

The pace at which artificial intelligence and big data are ruling the current world is simply incredible. The best example can be seen when you move from one region to another. When you see a YouTube video, you must have noticed that there are advertisements.

You will be surprised to notice that these advertisements are always shown according to the region in which you currently are. You will never get advertisements in German when you are in New York - unless, of course, you are from Germany - in which case, Google manages to tailor product offerings that might interest you - even in German.

Your smartphone tracks your position and updates it, and if advertisers choose geo specific locations to advertise, you wouldn't get German ads while in New York.

Every company has now got data analysts pitching for their product in every possible way. YouTube advertisements are also a part of this. When it is detected that you are in an English speaking region, it begins to show you advertisements in English - even if you do not know that language. Nothing can escape the attention of careful data analysts and their equally efficiently programmed analysis tool.

With such a vast effect on how we carry out business, Power Query is definitely the pillar of future data analytics. It will allow anyone and everyone concerned with collection, study, analysis and interpretation of data. It will allow the business decision makers to experiment with any new product or scheme with minimum risk.

With better access to accurate data, businesses can make the right decisions and leverage in on growth faster. That's one reason startups can't ignore Power Query.

They can even garner more revenue just from the likes, comments and shares from their social networking sites. It can be comfortably said that the rise of Power Query will lead to the sleeper success phenomenon where many companies may not be in direct profit through the sale of their products, but in indirect profits through their catchy advertisement campaigns.

As for the traditional business enterprises, Power Query will prove to be a boon. Currently, the role of data analysts or business analysts is much limited. They are concerned only with the decision making. But in the coming time, they will have a bigger role to play.

They can pitch for better advertisement campaigns through a well-documented research on the likes and dislikes of the population; can work in the hiring process by sorting out the candidates based on their LinkedIn profiles and the list is endless. The magnitude of change that Power Query is going to bring is unlimited.

As for example, we all know that LinkedIn and Glassdoor are currently the best online job portals. Now, if a company wishes to find best candidates for its job position, it can also employ Power Query here.

The data will be edited and polished in Query Editor to meet the company's requirements. Candidates can be sorted out on the basis of their educational qualifications and previous experience just like the normal edits. This will leave the company with a list of best candidates to be hired. The time and expenditure that was earlier used in the whole recruitment process will be decreased by several times. Thus, Power Query will rule the recruitment world too.

Currently, there is an ever-growing percentage of companies that are pitching for more use of Power Query in their firm. As for a data source, currently, 45,000 companies are employing Power Query for better data collection, differentiation and analysis. This can free them from the hassles of installing separate servers and software. Many resources need to be invested in their maintenance too.

The mobility of the employees was limited. But with the introduction of Power Query, all these factors have simply vanished. Companies do not need to maintain such expensive servers. All the information I snow stored in the cloud. This has led to more mobility of the employees. This is the reason that most companies now pitch for work from home options.

The best part of Power Query is that unlike previous data analytical tools that needed a specific programming language to be learnt for proper use, it is fit to be used even for a non-technical person. Except for the customized column creation feature, the whole of the Power Query is pretty user-friendly.

It needs no extra knowledge of any programming or query language. Even a person with the basic knowledge of MS-Excel can sign into this tool and gain insightful views over the various online data sheets and use them for further analysis. Its outreach can be understood by its statistics itself. Nearly 1 million users around the world are currently using Power Query for various data analytical purposes.

Going by this figure, it will be a matter of a couple of years, in which almost all the business enterprises will be utilizing Power Query for one or the other purpose.

One of the best user-friendly features that have been introduced in these data analytical tools is their mobile-friendly versions.

This allows the users to access the data from anywhere and then perform the required function with just a few touches. Its user-friendly version allows even the businessmen to access their business data sheets and derive the various outcomes without the help from any business analyst. This has in fact given them more control over their operations and certainly more freedom.

Power Query also allows for continuous refreshing of the data. It means that if you have put a function over a particular data sheet that changes after every transaction, then by simply clicking the refresh options, you can update the table. This feature is especially helpful for those who are involved in online businesses. Also, those who are operating facebook business pages or YouTube channels will benefit from this feature. Keeping track of the visitors on a Facebook page or any other online platform is very tough. It changes every second and does not follow any particular pattern.

In such a scenario, manually entering the updated data after every hour will be very tedious and definitely susceptible to human errors. However, with the refresh query feature of Power Query, these can be handled efficiently.

Microsoft is continuously working to upgrade the data analytics for everyone who uses Power BI. Since it is easily adaptable with Azure HDinsight, Hadoop and many other Big Data programs, its use across the various platforms is highly projected. So anyone who wants to learn data analytics to gain more insight into their business operations should surely get familiar with Power Query. It is going to be the future of business operations.

--

Conclusion

Thank you again for downloading this book!

I hope this book was able to help you .

Finally, if you enjoyed this book, then I'd like to ask you for a favor, would you be kind enough to leave a review for this book on Amazon? It'd be greatly appreciated!

Below you'll find some of my other popular books that are popular on Amazon . Simply click on the links below to check them out.

https://www.amazon.com/dp/B07BDKHGW5

www.ingramcontent.com/pod-product-compliance
Lightning Source LLC
Chambersburg PA
CBHW071553080326
40690CB00056B/1811